Violoncello

Gabriel Koeppen

Talking Strings

22 Solo pieces in popular style
22 Solostücke in populärer Stilistik
for Cello / für Cello

Coverillustration: Katharina Madesta

ED 23726
ISMN 979-0-001-21834-4

www.schott-music.com

Mainz · London · Madrid · Paris · New York · Tokyo · Beijing

Contents / Inhalt

Teil 1 / Part 1

Teil 2 / Part 2

Preface

The pieces in this booklet were written between 2002 and 2004 and initially published in two volumes by „Edition Gabricelli". This new edition brings together all the pieces in one volume. My aim was to write new solo pieces for auditions and concerts that would bring a breath of fresh air to the teaching repertoire and make practising fun. The result is a colourful mixture of classical, jazz, folk, rock, and pop music. The pieces can be freely arranged into small groups or suites for auditions and concerts.

The pieces are in rough order of difficulty. Part 1 contains easier pieces with a difficulty level of 3–5, part 2 is technically much more demanding and is aimed at advanced pupils and students. However, professional cellists may also find interesting concert pieces here (grades 5–7).

Special playing techniques usually are explained in footnotes, sometimes with additional exercises at the end of the piece. Modern playing techniques such as percussion on the cello, ghost notes (muted notes), slides, improvisation interludes, imitation of a distorted electric guitar, etc. sometimes make the notation a little more complicated. I hope that I have succeeded in notating everything clearly.

Please let your imagination run free and add your own introductions and postludes or small improvisations or variations to the pieces.

My special thanks go to all the students and colleagues who were involved in the creative process and without whom the book would not be available in this form.

Enjoy practising and performing!

Gabriel Koeppen

Vorwort

Die Stücke in diesem Heft entstanden in den Jahren 2002 bis 2004 und erschienen zunächst in zwei Bänden im Verlag „Edition Gabricelli". Die vorliegende Neuausgabe fasst alle Stücke zu einem Band zusammen. Mein Ziel war es, neue Solostücke für Vorspiel und Konzert zu schreiben, die „frischen Wind" ins Unterrichtsrepertoire bringen und bei denen das Üben Spaß macht. Herausgekommen ist dabei eine bunte Mischung aus Klassik, Jazz, Folk, Rock und Pop. Die Stücke können im Vorspiel und Konzert gerne zu kleinen Gruppen oder Suiten frei zusammengestellt werden.

Die Stücke sind grob nach Schwierigkeit geordnet. Teil 1 enthält einfachere Stücke im Schwierigkeitsgrad 2–3, Teil 2 ist technisch deutlich anspruchsvoller und wendet sich an fortgeschrittene Schüler und Studenten, aber auch professionelle Cellist:innen werden hier vielleicht interessante Vortragsstücke finden (Schwierigkeitsgrad 3–4).

Besondere Spieltechniken werden meist mit Fußnoten erklärt, manchmal auch durch Zusatzübungen am Ende des Stückes. Moderne Spieltechniken wie Percussion auf dem Cello, Ghost Notes (abgedämpfte Töne), Slides, Improvisationseinlagen, Imitation einer verzerrten E-Gitarre etc. machen die Notation manchmal etwas komplizierter. Ich hoffe, dass es gelungen ist, alles verständlich zu notieren.

Die Interpret:innen können ihrer Fantasie freien Lauf lassen und die Stücke durch eigene Vor- und Nachspiele oder durch kleine eingefügte Improvisationen oder Variationen ergänzen.

Mein besonderer Dank gilt allen Schüler:innen und Kollegen:innen, die am Prozess der Entstehung beteiligt waren und ohne die das Heft in dieser Form nicht vorliegen würde.

Ich wünsche viel Spaß beim Üben und Vorspielen.

Gabriel Koeppen

Part 1 / Teil 1

1 Nobody's perfect

Gabriel Koeppen
*1958

*) The small notes can be omitted. / Die kleinen Noten können weggelassen werden.

2 Little Tango / Kleiner Tango

Gabriel Koeppen

3 Prelude in C major / Präludium C-Dur

Gabriel Koeppen

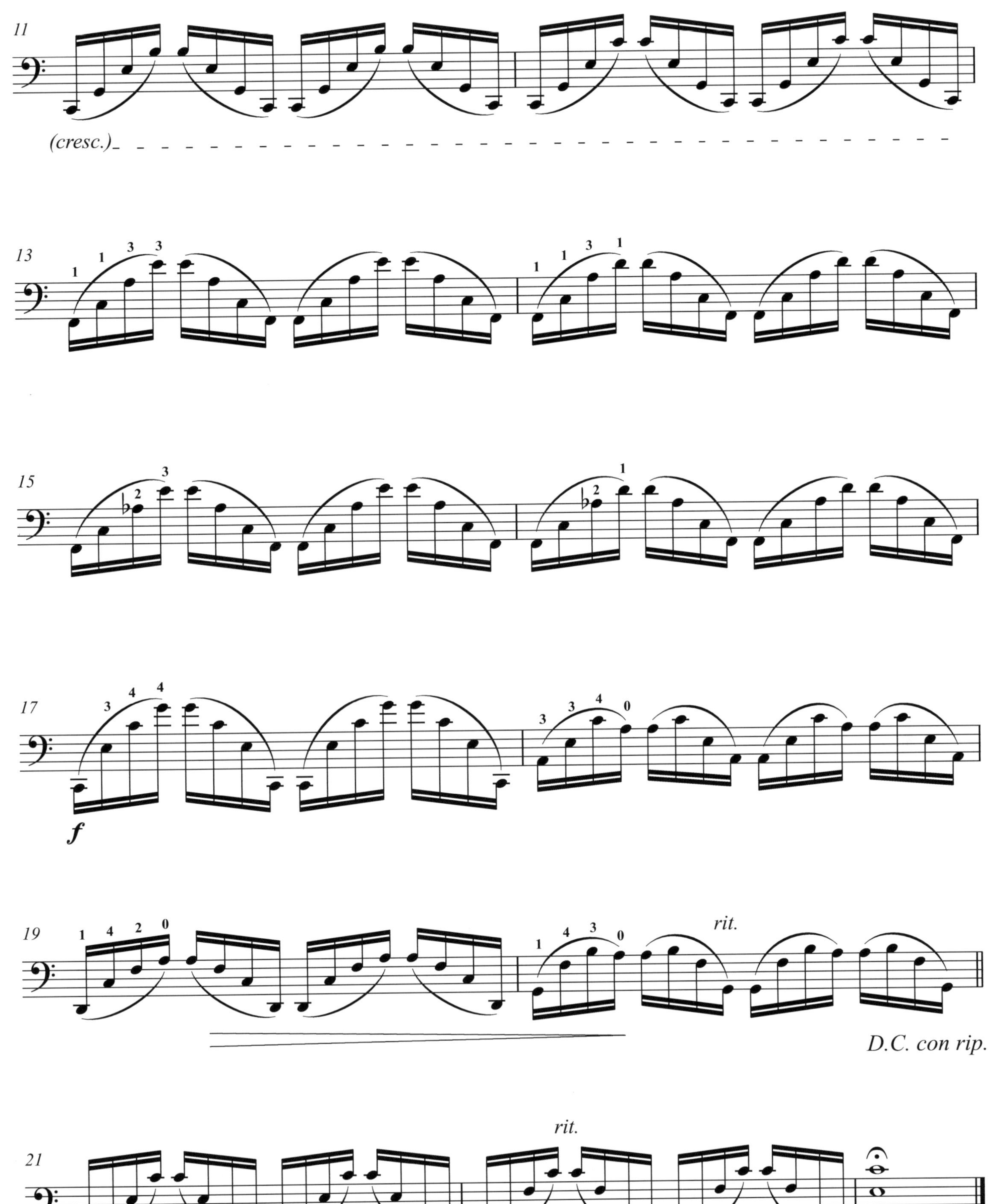

11
(cresc.)
13
15
17
f
19
rit.
D.C. con rip.
21
rit.
p

4 Desert ride / Wüstenritt

Gabriel Koeppen

5 Bullfiddle

Gabriel Koeppen

Cheerful / Fröhlich (𝅗𝅥 = 92–112)

mf

cresc.

accelerando poco a poco

f

1.

2.

molto accelerando

f

p

sfz

*) Slide = short glissando / kurzes Glissando

6 Dr. Jekyll and Mr. Hyde

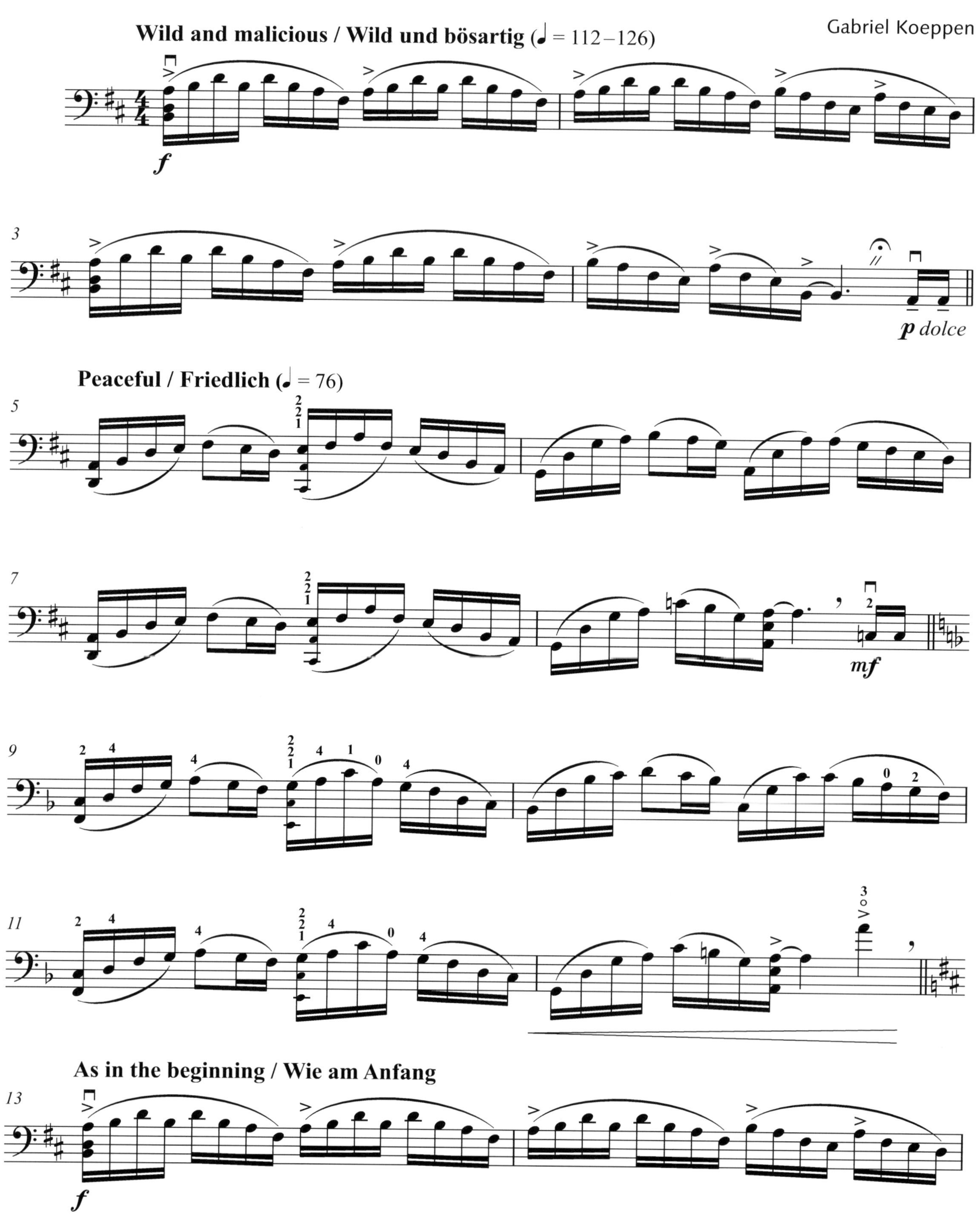

15
17
19
ff
sfz

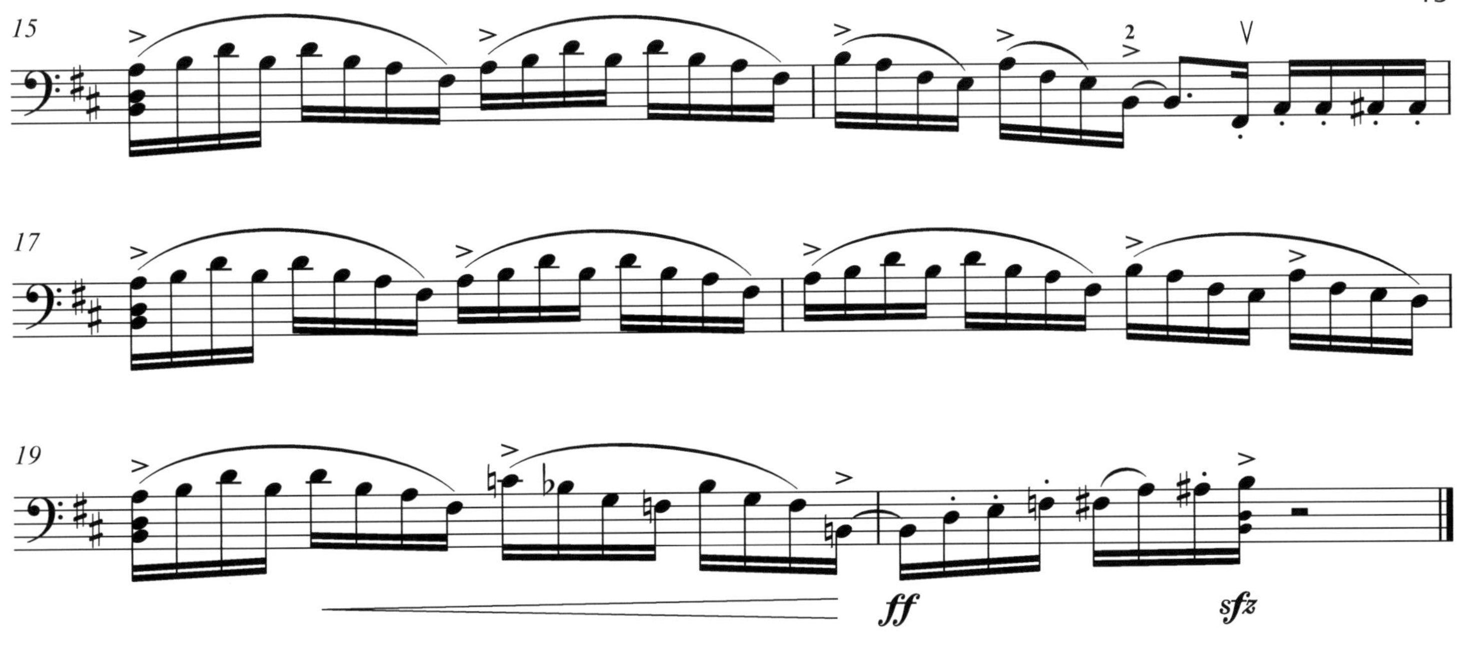

7 Night mood / Nachtstimmung

Very slow / Sehr langsam (♩ = 52)

Gabriel Koeppen

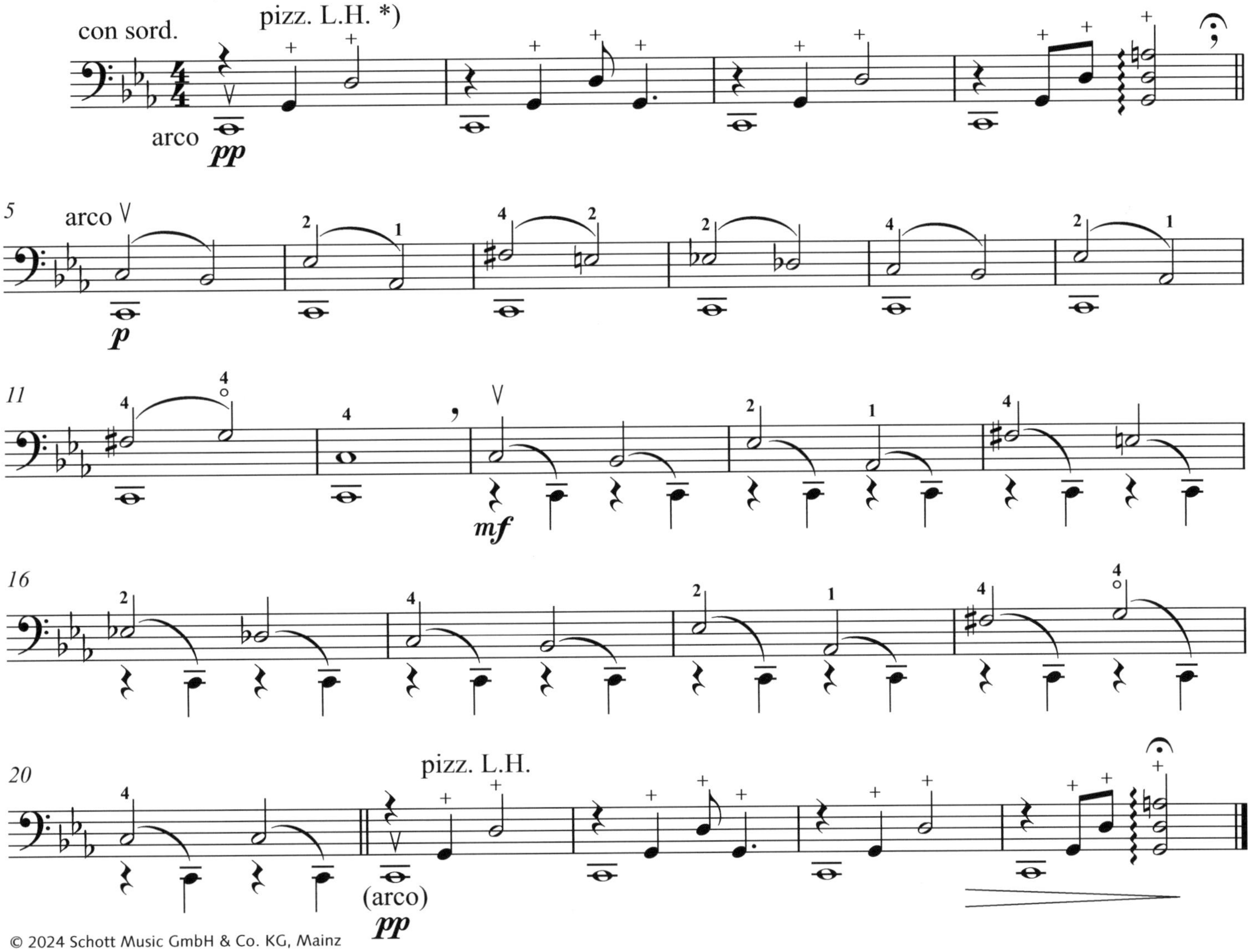

con sord.
pizz. L.H. *)
arco
pp
5
arco
p
11
mf
16
20
pizz. L.H.
(arco)
pp

*) Pluck with the left hand / mit der linken Hand zupfen

8 Loneliness / Einsamkeit

Gabriel Koeppen

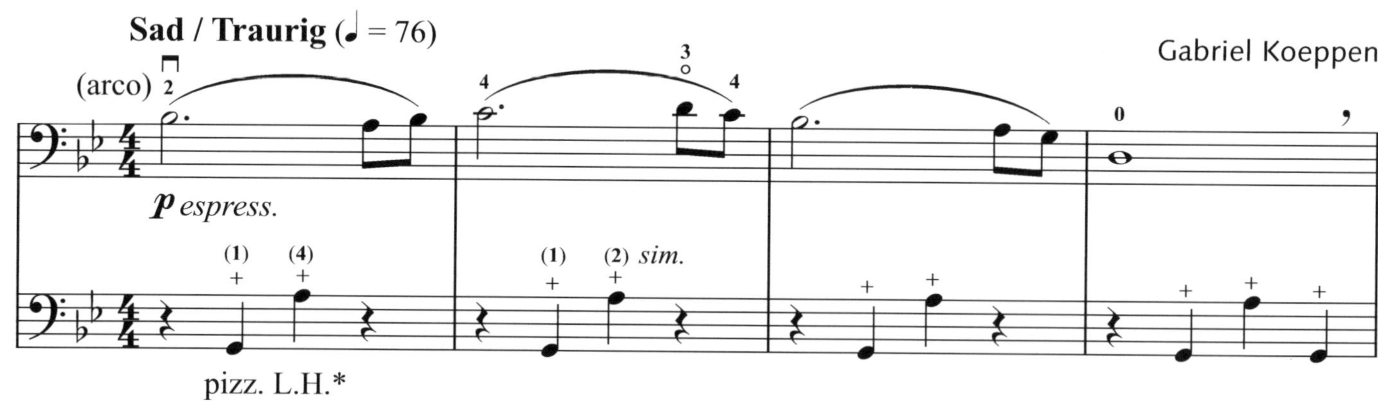

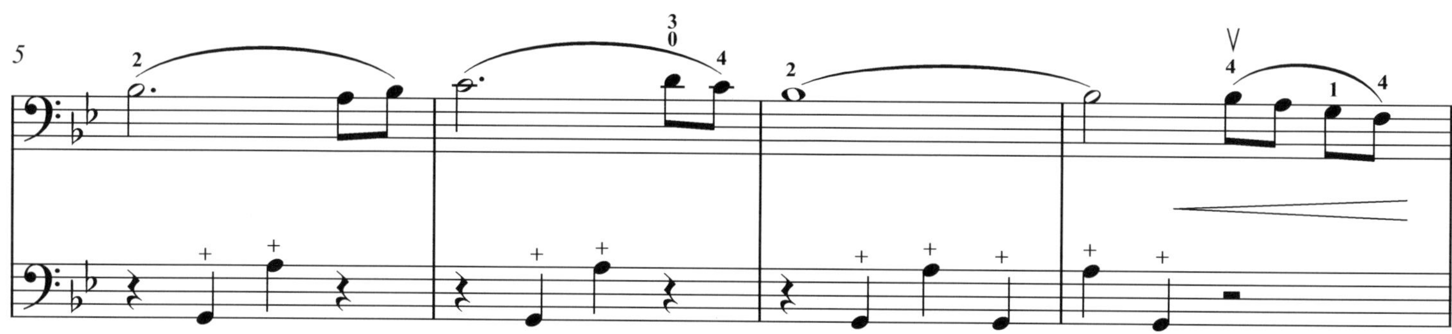

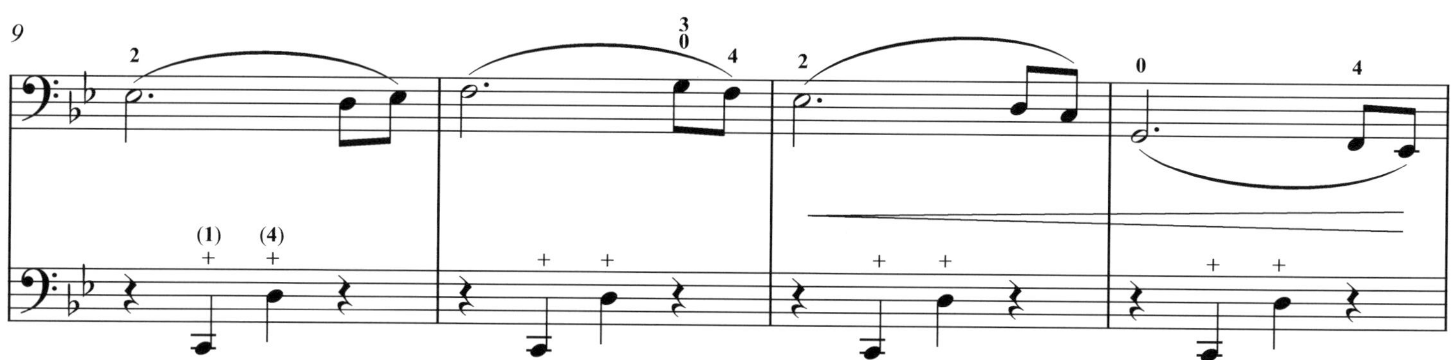

*) Always pluck with your left hand. The fingerings in brackets indicate which finger is used for pizzicato. / Immer mit der linken Hand zupfen. Die Fingersätze in Klammern geben an, mit welchem Finger gezupft wird.

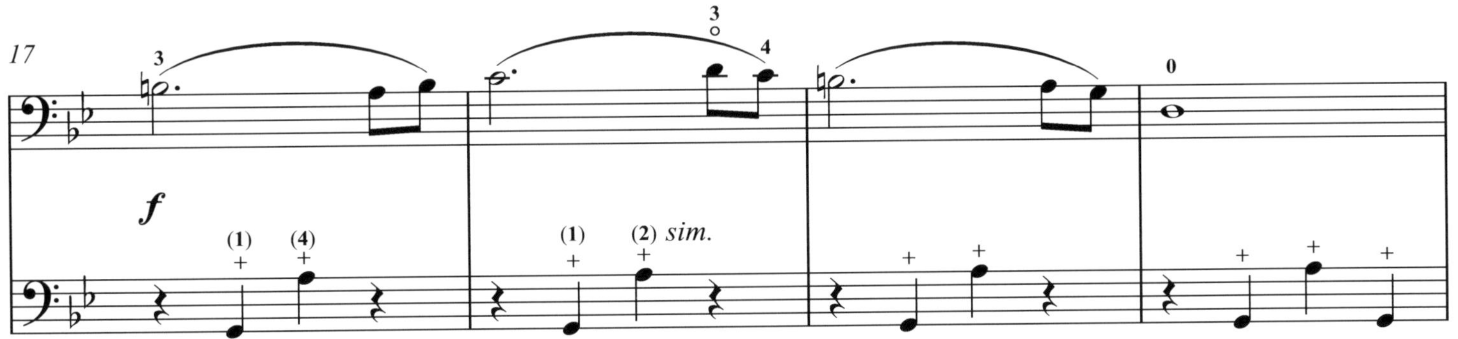

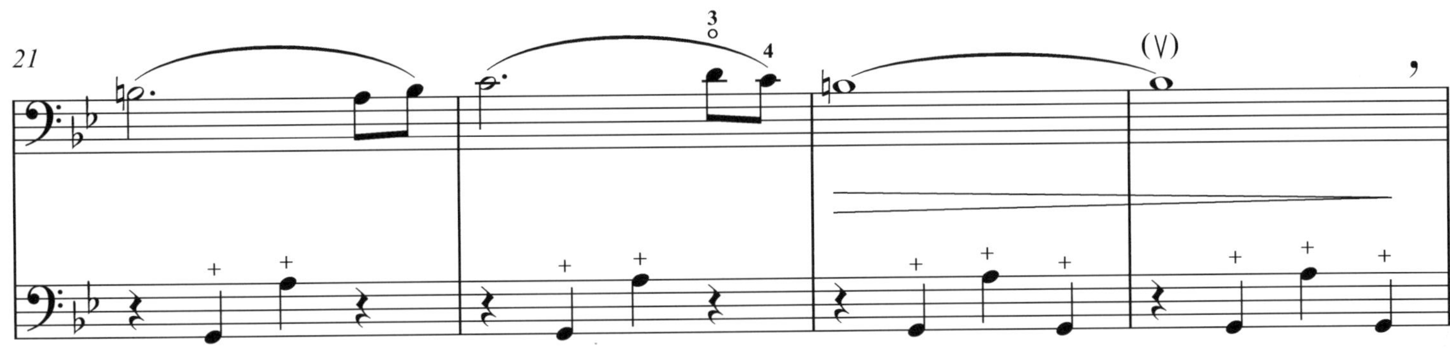

Meno mosso

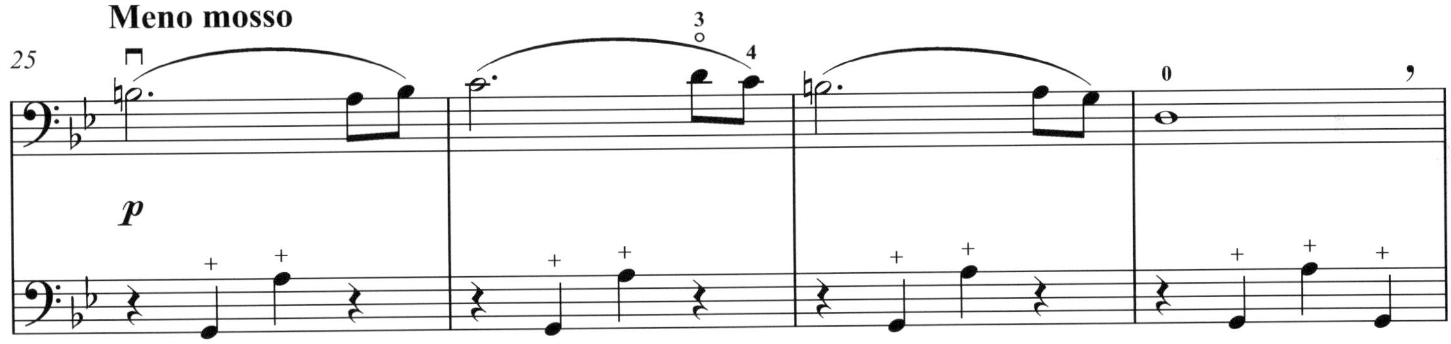

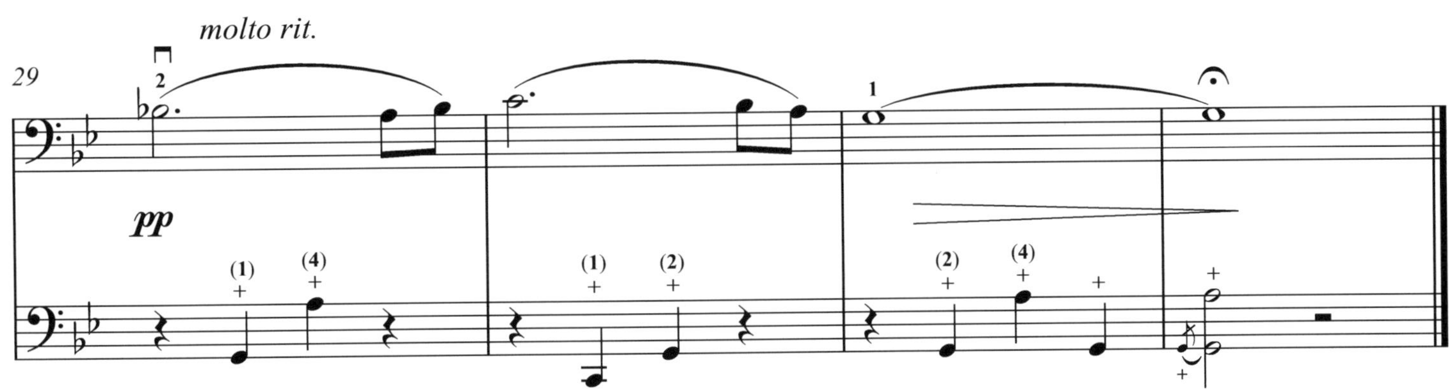

9 Go home!

Gabriel Koeppen

10 Fata Morgana

Not fast / Nicht schnell (♩ = 96)

Rip. sul pont.

Gabriel Koeppen

11 Pizz-a

Gabriel Koeppen

*) Fingerpicking: pluck with thumb (D), index finger (1) and middle finger (2) like on a guitar: the thumb plucks the bass part, the 1st finger the D-string and the 2nd finger the A-string. Hold the chord fingerings as long as possible and let them sound. Ties are played by hammering, plucking or gliss. with the left hand. / Fingerpicking: mit Daumen (D), Zeigefinger (1) und Mittelfinger (2) zupfen wie auf einer Gitarre. Der Daumen zupft die Bassstimme, der 1. Finger die D-Saite und der 2. Finger die A-Saite. Akkorde möglichst lange halten und klingen lassen. Bindungen werden durch Hämmern, Abzupfen oder gliss. mit der linken Hand erzeugt.

12 Stand up!

Gabriel Koeppen

Part 2 / Teil 2

13 Prelude in D major / Präludium D-Dur

Gabriel Koeppen

cresc.
1.
f pesante
tr
f
2.
cresc.
tr
f pesante
tr
rit.
ff

14 Expedition

*) Pizz. as a percussive effect, binding by damping with the left hand (ghost notes). The A-string may also sound. / Pizz. als perkussiver Effekt, Bindung durch Abdämpfen mit der linken Hand (ghost notes). Die A-Saite darf mitklingen.
**) Slide = short glissando / kurzes Glissando

24
26
poco rit.
29
p
sim.
32
35
38
decresc.
41
44
pp
47
pizz.*)
pizz.
mf / f
rit.

15 Northern city cowboy

15
pp
17
1.
2.
mf
f
2nd time faster / 2. Mal schneller
19
f
sfz
21
23
25
1.
2.
gliss.
pizz.

16 Little romance / Kleine Romanze

Gabriel Koeppen

21
23
25
cresc.
27
rit.
Tempo I
f
p
30
IV III II III
II III
33
rit.
pp
III
IV

17 If I would...

Gabriel Koeppen

(26)
♩ = 92 – 108
f
29
4
31
2
1
0
4
33
0
1
0
1
Tempo I
35
f marcato
2
0
39
decresc.
43
molto rit.
sfz

18 Let´s go

Gabriel Koeppen

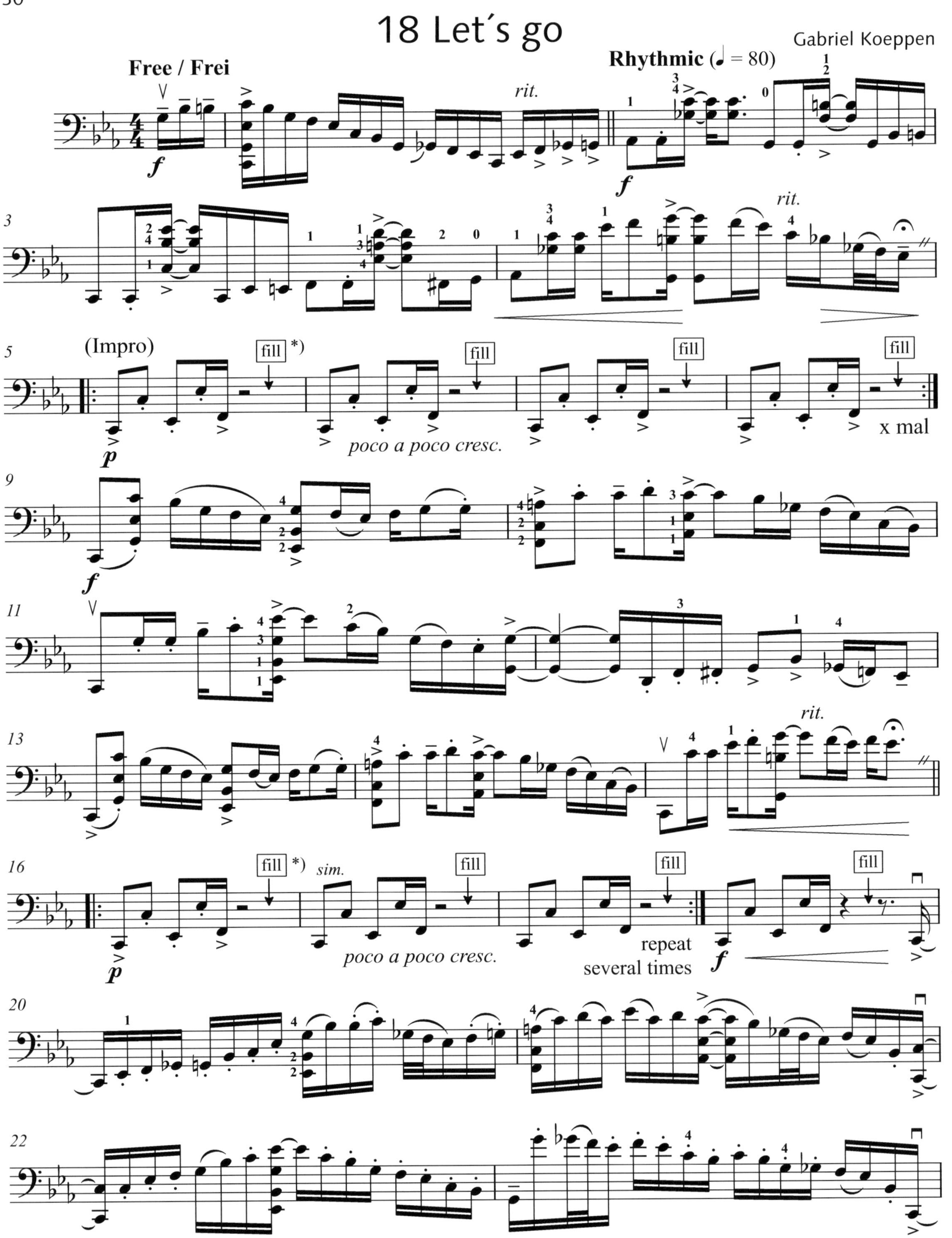

*) Fill the half breaks with short improvisations (fills). Combine and vary the fills and invent your own. Also experiment with harmonics. / Spiele in den halben Pausen kurze Improvisationen (Fills). Kombiniere und variiere die Fills und erfinde eigene. Experimentiere auch mit Flageoletts.

24
25
26
rit.
27
fill
fill
fill
fill
p
decresc.
repeat and fade

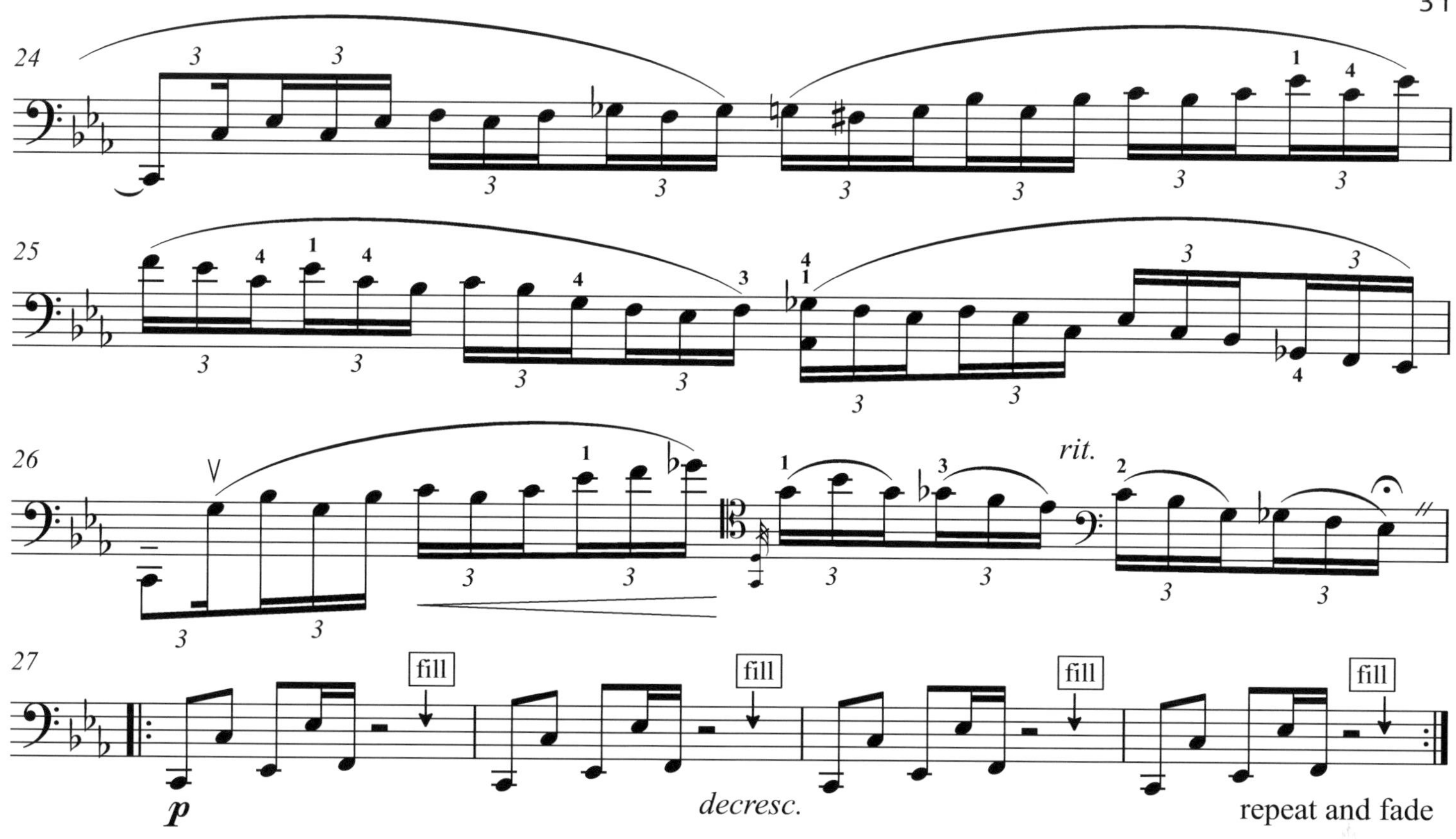

Percussive fills: e.g. hitting the rib or body with fingers or the flat of the left hand, bowing on the side of the bridge, tapping the neck with a knuckle, bowing muted strings, col legno, rubbing on the top etc. /
Perkussive Fills: z. B. mit Fingern oder der flachen linken Hand auf Zarge oder Korpus schlagen, auf der Seite des Stegs streichen, mit einem Fingerknöchel am Hals klopfen, abgedämpfte Saiten streichen, col legno, auf der Decke reiben etc.

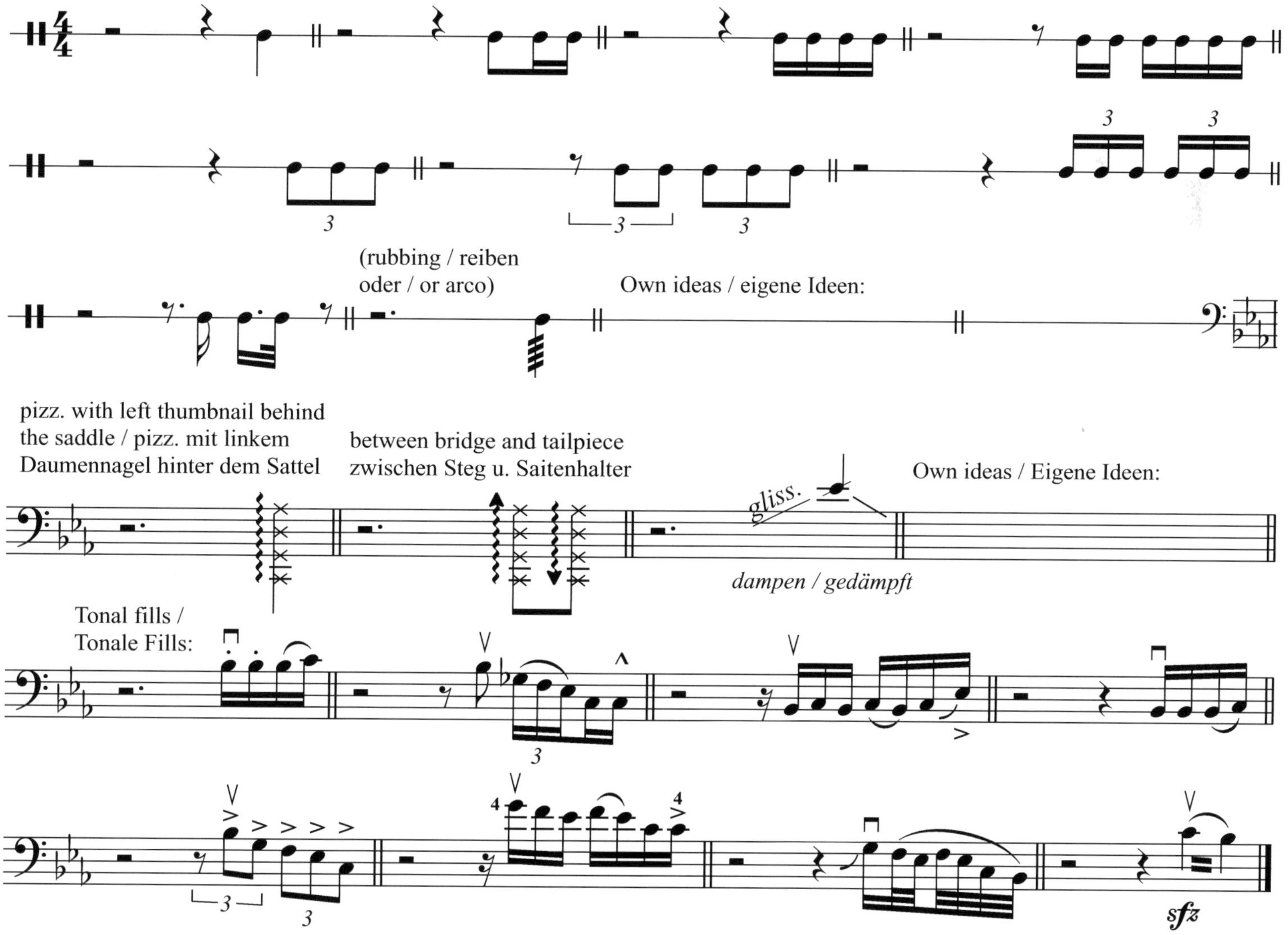

(rubbing / reiben oder / or arco)
Own ideas / eigene Ideen:
pizz. with left thumbnail behind the saddle / pizz. mit linkem Daumennagel hinter dem Sattel
between bridge and tailpiece zwischen Steg u. Saitenhalter
gliss.
Own ideas / Eigene Ideen:
dampen / gedämpft
Tonal fills / Tonale Fills:
sfz

19 Sunset at the sea

Gabriel Koeppen

*) Let the chords ring / Akkorde klingen lassen

molto rit.
Tempo I
p espress.
rit.
rubato
pizz.
p
rit.

20 Wacky / Abgedreht

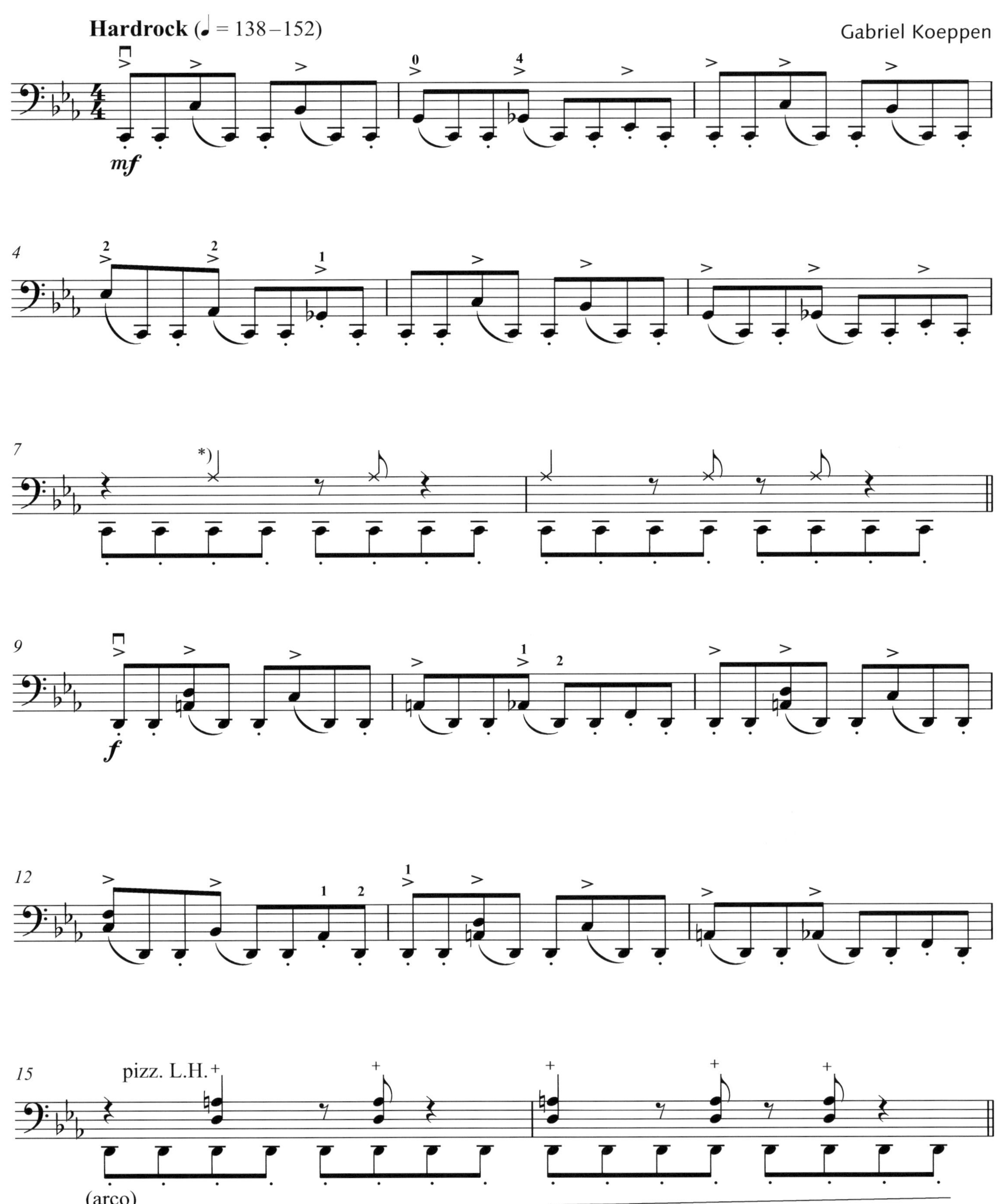

*) Tap on the rib or the top with your left hand / mit der linken Hand auf Zarge oder Decke klopfen

17
più f
(2 4)
19
22
ff
II
III
24
II
III
26
I
II
28
1.
gliss.
2.
gliss.
ff
sfz

21 Thinking / Nachdenklich

Gabriel Koeppen

cresc.
f
rit.
Tempo I
mf
p
rit.
II
III
pp

22 Tribute to Jimi Hendrix

Gabriel Koeppen

*) Dampen with the left hand by loosening the previous grip (ghost notes) /
Mit der linken Hand abdämpfen durch Lockern des vorherigen Griffes (ghost notes)

*) Remain in thumb position and damp with the left index finger / In der Daumenlage bleiben und mit dem linken Zeigefinger abdämpfen
**) Tap on the top with L.H. / mit der L.H. auf die Decke schlagen